THE MIDEAST AFTER THE

GULF WAR

Richard Steins

THE MILLBROOK PRESS

Brookfield, Connecticut

Published by The Millbrook Press
2 Old New Milford Road
Brookfield, CT 06804
© 1992 Blackbirch Graphics, Inc.
First Edition

Created and produced in association with Blackbirch Graphics.
Series Editor: Bruce S. Glassman

Library of Congress Cataloging-in-Publication Data
Steins, Richard.
    The Mideast after the Gulf war/Richard Steins.
    Includes bibliographical references and index.
    Summary: Provides information and background on the Mideast after the
1991 Persian Gulf War, including refugee problems, environmental damage,
and unsettled political situations.
    1. Middle East—Politics and government—1979. 2. Persian Gulf War,
1991—Influence. I. Title. II. Series.
ISBN 1-56294-156-9
DS63.1.S74   1992
9456.704'3—dc20   91-29944
                                                            CIP
                                                            AC

Contents

Chapter 1

Surrender in the Desert

At exactly 9 p.m. on Thursday, February 28, 1991, President George Bush went on television and announced to the American people that "Kuwait is liberated."

After six weeks of heavy air raids on Iraq and only one hundred hours of infantry and tank fighting on the ground, the U.S.-led Operation Desert Storm was over. The Iraqi army of President Saddam Hussein, which seven months before had stormed into neighboring Kuwait, had been crushed by the allies. The capital of Kuwait City was now occupied by the victorious forces. The citizens of Kuwait danced with joy in the streets and showered the American soldiers with flowers and other gifts.

In his speech, President Bush called on the Iraqis to meet with the allied officers somewhere in the war zone within the next forty-eight hours to settle on the terms of a cease-fire.

Cease-Fire at Safwan

The meeting—to arrange the cease-fire—was really a surrender in the desert. The allies chose an airfield in the Iraqi desert near Safwan for the site of the meeting.

The American general, H. Norman Schwarzkopf, leader of the allied coalition, arrived for the meeting in a squadron

> The citizens of Kuwait danced with joy in the streets

Opposite:
An Iraqi soldier waves a piece of white paper as he surrenders to an allied soldier.

On Thursday, February 28, 1991, U.S. President George Bush announced an official cease-fire in the Persian Gulf.

of six Apache attack helicopters. The Iraqi general, Lieutenant General Sultan Hashim Ahmed, was escorted to the meeting by allied soldiers driving in standard U.S. Army open-air jeeps.

The airfield was ringed by more than fifty allied tanks and armored vehicles draped with American and British

THE GROUND WAR STRATEGY

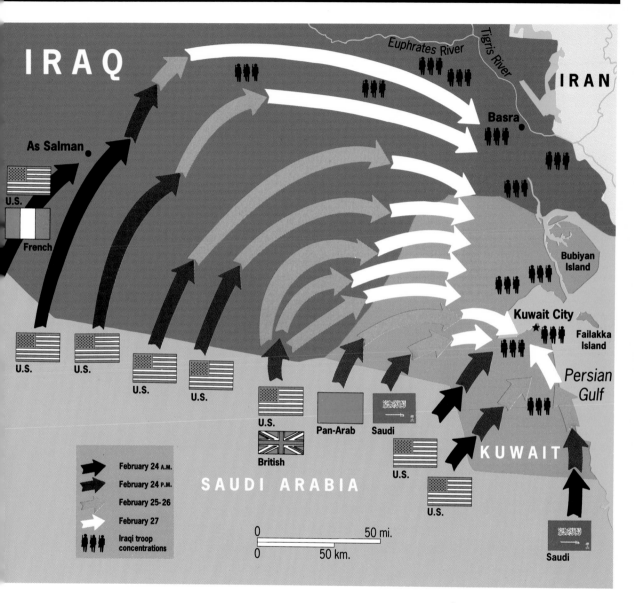

flags. As the Iraqis arrived, there was no mistake who had won the war.

Inside a green army tent, General Ahmed was shown to a seat at a plain wooden table, facing a grim-faced General Schwarzkopf. The Iraqis smiled nervously, but the Americans did not return the smiles or engage in small talk.

American General H. Norman Schwarzkopf hugs the Kuwaiti commander-in-chief, Jabar-al-Sabah, before the cease-fire meeting in Iraq.

Within two hours, the Iraqi delegation had accepted all of the allies' terms for a temporary cease-fire. The Iraqi army would cease all resistance to the allies and return to Iraq without its weapons. What was left of the Iraqi air force—especially fixed-wing aircraft—was forbidden to fly over Iraqi territory.

After the Iraqis had signed the agreement, General Schwarzkopf then walked General Ahmed back to the jeep that had brought him to the meeting. Only at that point did the American salute the Iraqi and shake his hand. The fighting was officially over. Soon, allied troops would begin the process of returning home to their families.

The Threats That Never Were

From the very start of the Persian Gulf crisis, U.S. military analysts were quick to raise concerns about the potential threats of the Iraqi arsenal. Many warned repeatedly about hidden forces, unknown power, and secret weapons.

Most analysts agreed that the allies faced four major obstacles. But these dangers never materialized. What happened to the threats that never were?

Air Defenses

 At the start of the war, the Iraqi skies were protected by an air force of approximately eight hundred combat planes. In addition to planes, the Iraqis possessed thousands of anti-aircraft missiles and artillery pieces. Even though these forces appeared to be a more serious threat than those that destroyed hundreds of American aircraft in Vietnam, they proved to be almost completely inneffective. In total, only thirty-six allied planes were shot down. The Pentagon had expected to lose over two hundred.

After losing thirty-six of his combat aircraft in the first few days of the war, Saddam Hussein sent most of his remaining best planes to Iran and grounded the rest of his air force. Allied jamming of electronics and radar rendered useless the Iraqi tracking facilities on the ground. The Iraqi anti-aircraft guns and missiles, though they filled the sky with dramatic fireworks displays, were firing blindly and were little threat to allied air forces.

Chemical Weapons

 Before the ground war began, allied forces were worried that Iraqi artillery might shoot poison and nerve gases. As it turned out, not one chemical weapon was fired during the entire course of the war. And it wasn't for lack of an arsenal that Iraq held back; U.S. Marines found large stores of poison-gas shells poised in frontline positions.

General Schwarzkopf said that he was unsure of why the Iraqis never unleashed their chemical weapons. He speculated that the Iraqi artillery that was needed to deliver the chemical weapons was too badly damaged to mount an effective assault. Another factor that most likely deterred the use of chemical weapons was the weather. Many of the days during the ground war were rainy and windy, and in most cases the wind was blowing from the south. During these days, any chemicals or gases released into the air would have blown right back onto the Iraqi forces.

The Front Line

 With months to build their fortifications deep into the sand, the Iraqi army was "dug in" well before the ground war began. In the days before the allied ground assault, many feared that the Iraqi front line would be a tough wall to break through; one that could result in heavy casualties for both sides. Iraq had built bunkers, sowed minefields, and camouflaged ditches filled with oil. This strategy was supposed to channel the advancing forces into designated areas, or "killing zones," where heavily built-up Iraqi artillery would decimate oncoming troops.

The Iraqis, however, did not count on allied forces outflanking their "corridors of death." As some coalition forces went around these fortified areas, others penetrated directly. These forces found mostly unattended barricades and abandoned fortifications. Much of the front line had been deserted by war-weary, undernourished, and despondent Iraqi soldiers who were thrilled to surrender.

The Republican Guard

 The Republican Guard—over 125,000 strong—was supposed to be one of Saddam Hussein's "trump cards." The word from military analysts was that the nine divisions of the Guard were Iraq's best-trained, most fiercesome, and most elite fighting forces. Their function was to sit behind the front lines and to drive advancing forces back if they drove through Iraq's regular infantry. When the allied ground invasion began, however, Iraq's plan fell completely to pieces.

Coalition forces broke through Iraqi lines in various places along the Kuwait border, but Iraq's communication systems were nonfunctional. The Guard command had no idea where allied troops had advanced and no idea how to counterattack.

يا جابر الشعب يا نبض الحب   الشعب حماك والله يرعاك

Chapter 2

The Legacy of War

The majority of American people exploded with an unprecedented outpouring of national pride over the victory in the Persian Gulf War. Only months before, more than 400,000 American troops had been sent to the Mideast by President Bush to help liberate Kuwait and to protect that vital oil-rich region from the threat of Saddam Hussein.

The American public had strongly supported the president's policy, but they were also anxious. Most Americans still remembered the Vietnam War in the 1960s and 1970s. That war had ended in defeat, with the last Americans lifted by helicopter off the roof of the U.S. embassy in Saigon only hours before the country was overrun by Communist North Vietnam.

But the Persian Gulf War had ended in what seemed to be a clear-cut U.S. and allied victory. Throughout the country—from Los Angeles in the West to Washington and New York in the East—huge parades were organized to welcome home the first returning troops. In New York, in June, more than a million people lined the streets of lower Manhattan as the victors of Operation Desert Storm were showered with tons of ticker tape.

Heroes of the war became legends overnight. The big, blunt, and outspoken commander of allied forces, four-star

Americans were jubilant, but Baghdad and Kuwait City were in ruins

Opposite:
An image of Kuwait's emir shares space with Uncle Sam in Kuwait City.

Americans in Fort Campbell, Kentucky, celebrate the victory of returning troops.

General H. Norman Schwarzkopf, became a familiar face on American television. Whether announcing that his forces were prepared to "kick butt" or showing compassion for a homesick young marine, General Schwarzkopf came to embody the common sense "get on with the job" approach that was at the heart of the American involvement in the conflict.

Another figure who received instant fame and adulation was General Colin L. Powell. The first African American to hold the highest military position in the United States, General Powell impressed the public with his calm and articulate briefings. By the time the war was over, he was being mentioned as a possible Republican vice presidential candidate in 1992.

Four months after the war, a Time/CNN poll found that eighty-nine percent of Americans still felt proud

AMERICAN OPINION AFTER THE WAR

Do you think the U.S. should be playing the role of world policeman, fighting aggression wherever it occurs?

Yes | 21%
No | 75%

Does the American performance in the war give you more or less confidence in the following:

	More Confidence	Less Confidence
The U.S. military	93%	3%
The American presidency	86%	8%
The Republican party	65%	16%
The U.S. media	54%	34%
The Democratic party	41%	34%

Which of these are the lessons from the war with Iraq?

	A Lesson	Not a Lesson
The U.S. is still the greatest military power	86%	8%
The U.S. must increase its efforts to end the unrest in the Middle East	65%	16%
The U.S. should not hesitate to use military force to protect its interests around the world	54%	34%
Only the U.S. can take the lead in protecting democracy in the world	41%	34%

"Undecided" and "Not Sure" responses have been omitted.
Data based on a TIME/CNN pol taken March 7, 1991.

General Colin Powell receives the Medal of Freedom from President Bush in a ceremony at the White House.

Baghdad After the War

The American bombing of Baghdad had a strange precision about it. In the center of town, a huge television station was totally gutted. Across the street, the national museum stood unharmed despite six weeks of air attacks.

The National Palace and Ministry of Defense were hit by low-flying Cruise Tomahawk missiles launched from U.S. Navy ships hundreds of miles away in the Persian Gulf. So were the city's main post office, a conference center, and a number of telephone exchanges. Bridges over the Tigris and Euphrates rivers, which run through the city, were knocked out, effectively dividing the city in two.

A walk through some streets revealed nothing but bombed out buildings. A few blocks away were street markets selling vegetables and other merchandise. A few months after the war, buses were running and traffic was heavy as travelers sought to get from one side of the rivers to the other.

But the surface was deceptive. Despite the appearances of normal life throughout much of Baghdad, life was anything but normal. One of the main targets of the allied bombers and missiles were plants that generated electrical power.

Baghdad in the first months after the war was a city in which electricity existed for only half of the day. Water purification plants were unable to function and raw sewage flowed in the streets as people tried to cope. Heaps of garbage were a common sight in many Iraqi neighborhoods.

Because of the continuing U.N. sanctions on trade, food prices skyrocketed. Although a thriving black market soon appeared, many Iraqis could not afford the high prices. As a result, infant formula and high-protein foods became more and more scarce. A can of infant formula, which had cost $1 before the war, cost $50 on the black market.

On March 22, 1991, the U.N. lifted its embargo on humanitarian shipments of food to Iraq, but with the continuing embargo on foreign financial transactions and the ban on the sale of Iraqi oil, the country could not import the necessary amounts of food and medicine.

Poor sanitation led to epidemics of cholera, gastroenteritis, and typhoid—all diseases common in areas where the water is impure.

The bombing turned out to have serious long-range consequences. The attacks on vital nerve centers like the country's electrical grid led to serious health consequences in the months after the war. It was, as one visiting doctor said, a campaign of "bomb now, die later."

A young Iraqi boy stands with a plate of sausages among the devastation left by allied bombing raids in Baghdad.

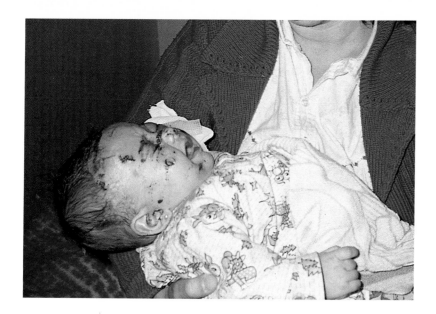

An injured Iraqi infant awaits attention at a hospital in Baghdad.

about what their country had accomplished in the conflict. But after the parades and the celebrations were over and the cheering had stopped, the question still had to be asked: Was it worth it?

Long-Range Consequences

The Persian Gulf War turned the Mideast upside down. Its immediate goals had been achieved. Kuwait was liberated, and Iraq, which lost three-fourths of its army, was eliminated as a threat to its neighbors.

In human terms, the war was devastating. Perhaps 100,000 Iraqi soldiers had been killed (the exact figure is not known). Iraq had been severely bombed, with most of its electrical and telecommunication systems, roads, and bridges severely damaged. Civilian casualties were thought to be high, with estimates between 1,500 and 15,000 killed. Some 7,000 Kuwaitis had died during the occupation. Kuwait had been looted by the Iraqis, who had also set ablaze 640 Kuwaiti oil wells. In addition to the pollution caused by these massive fires, the Persian Gulf was awash with some 500 million gallons of oil intentionally spilled by the Iraqis after the war broke out.

The news media were strictly controlled by the military during the war.

The long-range consequences were most difficult to understand at first. The war created an unusual alliance in which Arab fought Arab. The Gulf states—Saudi Arabia, the United Arab Emirates, Bahrain, Qatar, and Oman—joined the United States against their Arab brother Iraq.

So did the Arab state of Syria, a long time opponent of the United States, and Egypt, a strong U.S. ally in the region. Jordan, a moderate Arab state with good relations with the United States, finally wound up supporting Iraq. And the Palestine Liberation Organization (PLO), which claimed to speak for the millions of Palestinians scattered throughout the Mideast, supported Iraq.

The Media and the War

From the beginning of the bombing campaign against Iraq until the ceasefire in the desert six weeks later, American TV viewers saw one dramatic scene after another on the nightly news. Cameras placed in fighters recorded the deadly pinpoint accuracy of allied "smart bombs" as they struck Iraqi military targets. Live TV brought home the image of NBC correspondent Arthur Kent in Saudi Arabia pointing skyward as a Scud missile zeroed in on Riyadh. And reporters traveling with the allied forces sent back emotional pictures of joyful Kuwaitis greeting their liberators.

For the reporters on the scene, covering the Gulf War was a frustrating experience. The major complaint was that the U.S. government—through a variety of means and for a number of reasons—strictly controlled the flow of information about the war.

According to reporters and people in the media, the problems went far beyond censorship during the Persian Gulf War. The government, they charged, allowed some but not all information to come out, and at times slanted information in order to confuse the Iraqis. In short, the government managed the news for its own purposes.

One means of controlling information was to limit the number of reporters who could travel into battle zones. Those who could were forced to travel in pools and were escorted by military officers. By the time the ground war began, about two hundred reporters were traveling with the troops, but getting information back in a timely fashion proved difficult.

Another method of control was the use of daily press briefings by the military. At these briefings reporters were offered all kinds of statistics and were sometimes shown dramatic videos of successful allied bombings. However, because most people in the media were not allowed to travel to battle zones unescorted—and only one, Peter Arnett of CNN, had remained behind in Baghdad after others had been advised to leave by the U.S. government—they had no way of verifying many of the facts they were told.

As an example of deliberate deception, reporters could point to the coverage of allied training exercises for a landing on the shores of Kuwait from the sea. The U.S. encouraged the media to cover these exercises even though there was never any plan to launch a naval attack on Kuwait. The purpose of the coverage, according to many, was to use the media to intentionally deceive the Iraqis. In the final analysis, this deception proved successful. Some people say it even helped to win the war. Still, many people resented the fact that the true devastation of the war was not being shown.

After the war, opinion polls revealed that many Americans were angry with the media for their coverage of the conflict. Some people felt that a reporter like Arnett was playing into the hands of the Iraqis by showing the destruction caused by allied bombing. Others, however, felt that reporters had been all too eager to accept the government's version of what was happening. Many of the conflicts and tensions did not develop further because the war was over so quickly. Still, the fundamental issue of how freely the media can and should operate during wartime remained unresolved.

Peter Arnett CNN Reporting Baghdad, Iraq *Cleared by Iraqi Censors*

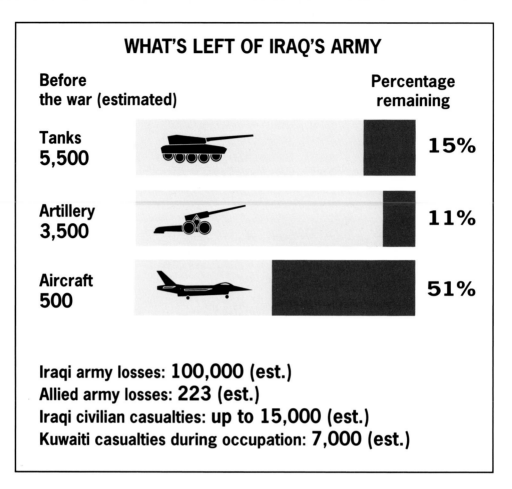

WHAT'S LEFT OF IRAQ'S ARMY

Before the war (estimated)

Percentage remaining

Tanks 5,500 — **15%**

Artillery 3,500 — **11%**

Aircraft 500 — **51%**

Iraqi army losses: **100,000 (est.)**
Allied army losses: **223 (est.)**
Iraqi civilian casualties: **up to 15,000 (est.)**
Kuwaiti casualties during occupation: **7,000 (est.)**

But the thirty-eight-nation coalition against Iraq included many countries outside the Mideast. The Americans provided the overwhelming number of ground troops and naval and air power, but soldiers from the Arab allies as well as from Great Britain, Italy, and France joined the battle as well. Significant economic aid was promised by Germany and Japan, whose constitutions did not permit their soldiers to fight in foreign wars. Saudi Arabia and the Kuwaiti government-in-exile also contributed millions of dollars in aid to support the war.

The main U.S. ally in the Mideast—and the strongest military power—was the Jewish state of Israel. When the conflict began, the Iraqis began firing Scud missiles into Israeli cities in order to terrorize the population. Yet the

Israelis, at U.S. urging, did not retaliate despite thirty-eight Scud attacks. If the Israelis joined the conflict, the United States was afraid that its Arab coalition partners would not want to be seen fighting on the same side as the Jewish state against an Arab country. Since Israel's founding in 1948, the only Arab state that has made peace with it has been Egypt. By staying on the sidelines, Israel helped the United States hold the fragile coalition together.

Although only some 148 Americans were killed in the war, the financial cost to Americans was staggering. One figure put the cost of the war at $47 billion. To help reduce the impact on American taxpayers, the United States asked its wealthiest allies to pay a portion of the bill.

Although the total count for Americans killed or wounded in the war was lower than expected, many soldiers were injured during the conflict.

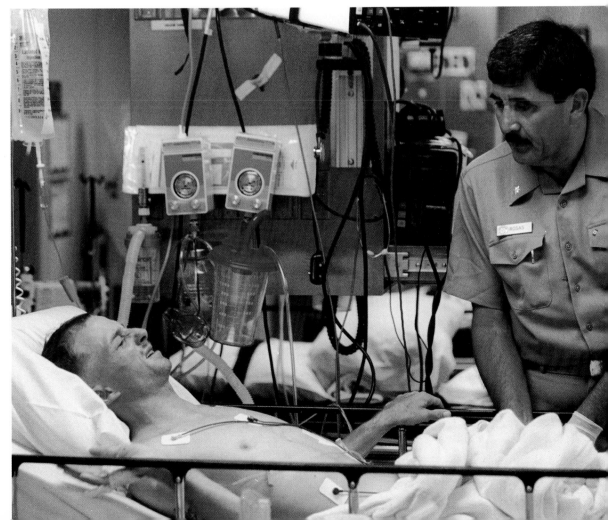

One Airman's Story

For a majority of the Americans sent to the Persian Gulf, the experience was both tense and boring. While awaiting orders to fight, they were constantly forced to clean their equipment from the effects of the desert sands. As they watched and waited, they thought of home and endured the blinding heat of day in the Arabian desert.

But for the pilots fighting the air war, combat began the moment the allies began bombing Iraq on January 17. The great majority returned to their bases unhurt after sorties over Baghdad and other cities. Some, however, were not so lucky.

Captain Richard D. Storr, an air force pilot, was flying his A-10 Warthog over Iraq on February 2 when it was struck by anti-aircraft fire. Storr tried until the last moment to save his crippled plane and return to safe air space over Kuwait, but just before crashing, he bailed out. He landed only five miles from the Kuwait border and was immediately captured by Iraqi soldiers. The Iraqis blindfolded him, shaved his head, and shipped him north to Baghdad. There, he was in a jail nicknamed the "Baghdad Biltmore." For twenty-one days Storr was held in solitary

confinement with only rice, beans, and water to eat. His captors questioned him constantly, beat him severely, and broke his nose.

On the night of February 23, American bombs struck the "Baghdad Biltmore." Storr's cell was reduced to rubble, but he survived the attack. He was then placed in a new cell with other prisoners, the first Americans he had seen in the three weeks of his captivity.

Storr was released on March 6, three days after the temporary cease-fire was signed at Safwan. His captivity had been frightening, but he had survived.

An American POW returns to Andrews Air Force Base after the war.

PAYING FOR THE WAR

	1990	1991 (projected)
U.S. cost	$11.1 billion	$36.4 billion
Allied pledges	– $9.7 billion	– $43.8 billion
	$1.4 billion Paid by U.S.	$7.4 billion Possible Surplus

Where the pledges come from (in millions)	Pledged to U.S. 1990*	Amount Received 1990*	Pledged to U.S. 1991*	Amount Received 1991*
Germany	$1,072	$803	$5,500	$2,160
Japan	1,740	1,323	9,000	0
Korea	80	71	305	0
Kuwait	2,506	2,506	13,500	1,004
Saudi Arabia	3,339	1,661	13,500	4,362
United Arab Emirates	1,000	981	2,000	29
Total	**$9,737**	**$7,345**	**$43,805**	**$7,555**

Source: Defense Budget Project   * in millions

Some wealthy Arab states—especially the Saudis and the Kuwaiti government-in-exile—pledged $35 billion. The Germans and the Japanese were pressured by the United States to contribute money to the war effort. Although they had been unable to participate directly in the war, their heavy dependence on foreign oil made it only fair that they help in any way possible.

After a period of lengthy debate, Japan finally agreed to contribute a total of $11 billion to the war effort, while the Germans pledged a total of $6.5 billion. The contribution of the allies to the war effort became a source of great irritation in the United States, particularly in the Congress. Many U.S. government leaders believed that the Germans and Japanese were not doing enough.

But perhaps the most far-reaching change brought about by the war was the increased influence of the United States in the Mideast. The United States emerged as the leading foreign power in the region. It now had a historic opportunity to use that influence to work for a permanent peace throughout the Mideast.

Liberated Kuwait

When the American and allied forces entered Kuwait City on February 27, 1991, they found a wrecked city and a wildly cheering population. As American tanks rolled down the streets, people chanted "Bush, Bush, Bush," in gratitude for what the United States had done. Seven months of Iraqi occupation had been a nightmare of death and destruction.

Kuwait in Ruins

Only a day before, the Iraqis had fled north toward their own border. In their hasty retreat, they stole everything that wasn't tied down and tried to destroy what was left behind. Virtually nothing in the country was untouched. Medicines, medical equipment, and beds were stolen from hospitals. Hotels lost furniture, rugs, and refrigerators. Business offices were plundered of computer terminals, which many Iraqi soldiers thought were television sets.

More than 3,200 gold bars worth about $700 million, were stolen from Kuwait's Central Bank, and some 350 million dinars (Kuwait's currency) worth of bank notes were also taken. The National Library lost 120,000 books. Priceless artistic and archaeological treasures were looted from Kuwait's museums.

Victory over Iraq was only the first step in rebuilding Kuwait

Opposite:
A Kuwaiti father and son wave their country's flag in Kuwait City the day their country was liberated.

A Kuwaiti mother is overcome with emotion as she returns to her homeland with her child in her arms.

Opposite:
Shop owner Mohammed Carsym stands in front of what was his Kuwait jewelry store. Shops that weren't destroyed were cleared out by looters.

Vehicles were particularly prized by the Iraqis. From all over Kuwait, more than 250,000 cars and trucks were stolen and taken back to Iraq.

Environmental destruction was catastrophic. During the course of the war, Iraq intentionally spilled almost 500 million gallons of oil into the Persian Gulf off Kuwait, the largest oil spill in history. The oil slick threatened the wildlife and coastline of Kuwait and neighboring Saudi Arabia, as well as water purification plants so vital to the desert region of the Arabian peninsula.

In addition, the Iraqis placed mines on almost all of Kuwait's one thousand oil wells. In their retreat, they blew up some 640 of these wells. The enormous black cloud from these burning wells threatened not only Kuwait but countries as far away as India.

The human toll during the war, however, was the greatest price paid by the Kuwaitis. During the occupation, thousands of Kuwaitis were tortured and murdered, especially any caught helping the Kuwaiti resistance. In the final days of the Iraqi retreat, an estimated forty thousand Kuwaiti civilians were kidnapped by the Iraqi forces and taken to Iraq. Almost all would eventually be returned to their native land in the following weeks.

Revenge

Before the Persian Gulf War, about seventy percent of the population of Kuwait were non-Kuwaitis. The Kuwaitis themselves were among the richest people in the world. The foreigners who lived in their country did the jobs that no Kuwaitis would do. They were laborers in the oil fields, maids, servants, truck drivers, clerks, and kitchen workers.

The largest group of non-Kuwaitis living in the country were the 400,000 Palestinians. Some had actually been born in Kuwait, while others had migrated there in search of work. Many had come from the Israeli-occupied West Bank after the Arab-Israeli War in 1967.

Although many Palestinians were opposed to the Iraqi invasion, and some had even fought in the resistance, the Palestine Liberation Organization (PLO) had supported Saddam Hussein.

After liberation, the Palestinians of Kuwait quickly became scapegoats. In March 1991, vigilante groups and even members of the Kuwaiti police forces hunted out Palestinians for revenge. Some one thousand were killed in the days immediately after the war. Although the government of Kuwait said it did not support such vengeful acts, government policy was to expel Palestinians from Kuwait, even if they had opposed Iraq's invasion. The old Arab way held that no matter where you live, you are what your parents or grandparents are. They believed in an old and rigid philosophy that says: Once a Palestinian, always a Palestinian.

Kuwait After the War

The quality of life in liberated Kuwait depended on one's nationality. Even though the country had been looted and destroyed by Iraqi troops, Kuwaitis could look forward to a return of self-government and the reconstruction of their country. For Palestinians living in Kuwait, however, the future was bleak.

The story of two Palestinians named Ali and Hasan are a case in point. Both came to Kuwait as young boys from the Israeli-occupied West Bank. Kuwait was the only home they had known.

As young adults, they were employed at Kuwait City's Plaza Hotel. After the Iraqi invasion, Ali and Hasan became active in the resistance. They moved money and guns around the city and helped Kuwaitis get fake Iraqi identity cards.

Just before the Iraqis withdrew, Ali and Hasan helped hide thirty-two women in a mosque to protect them from being raped by Iraqi troops.

With liberation, however, Ali and Hasan discovered that their heroism in the resistance mattered very little. The owner of the Plaza Hotel was a Kuwaiti, and he protected the young men from reprisals by the government. Unlike other Palestinians, they were allowed to keep their jobs. Most Palestinians were fired from their jobs and were deprived of free medical care and schooling. Returning Kuwaiti landlords were demanding back rent from their Palestinian tenants, but without income, they could not pay.

One of the hardest things for Ali and Hasan, however, was the loss of their Kuwaiti friends. Because the Palestine Liberation Organization had supported Iraq, all Palestinians were regarded as collaborators by the government of Kuwait. To be seen as a friend of a Palestinian could open one to a charge of collaborating with Iraq.

If all Palestinians are eventually expelled from Kuwait, the country will be a very different place from pre-invasion Kuwait. The 70-30 ratio of non-Kuwaitis to Kuwaitis is bound to come down. Even though Kuwaitis have traditionally been reluctant to take on low-paying jobs, more and more have been forced to perform duties usually reserved for Palestinians and foreign laborers.

The government of Kuwait set a goal of a 50-50 ratio in the years ahead. The new foreign workers are likely to be Asians. Only those Arabs whose countries did not support Saddam Hussein will be allowed to stay in the new Kuwait. In the meantime, the Palestinians remaining in Kuwait sit and wait, stateless people unwanted where they now live and unable to leave for a new home.

Kuwait City, May 1991.

After the invasion in August 1990, some 230,000 Palestinians had fled Kuwait. None were allowed to return. For those who remained behind, life became increasingly difficult. Although the vigilante groups were gradually brought under control, most of the remaining 170,000 Palestinians were fired from their jobs and deprived of free medical care and schooling.

Even leaving the country proved difficult. Some 30,000 Palestinians in Kuwait held Egyptian travel documents, but the government of Egypt refused to allow them to migrate. The only place to go was Jordan, but the government of Saudi Arabia refused to allow the Palestinians to travel over land. As a result, the Palestinians remaining in Kuwait were left with neither jobs nor anywhere to go.

Although the treatment of the Palestinians caused great concern around the world, the government of Kuwait seemed determined to expel them and any other foreign residents whose nationality was associated with countries that had supported the Iraqi invasion. The brutality of the invasion and the war had seriously shaken the Kuwaitis. No longer would they be complacent about their wealth or thriving economy. Now, they were not taking any chances.

In May, the government of Kuwait began holding trials of those accused of collaborating with Iraq. Most of the people put on trial were Palestinians from Jordan. By the summer of 1991 some thirty people had been sentenced to death, but the government of Kuwait postponed carrying out the sentences as many human rights groups and foreign governments protested the trials.

The Struggle for Democracy in Kuwait

Kuwait was founded in the 1700s and was governed by three families. One of these families—the Sabahs—are the current rulers and are led by Sheik Jabir al-Ahmed al-Sabah, the emir of Kuwait. Kuwaitis had traditionally been traders who sailed the Persian Gulf and sold their goods as far away as India.

But in the 1930s, oil was discovered. By the 1950s, Kuwait was exporting oil and becoming more and more wealthy. In 1961, Kuwait became independent from Great Britain, which had governed the region since 1899.

Before the Iraqi invasion, Kuwait had enjoyed some democratic freedoms, but the country was never democratic in the way the United States is. The Sabah family controlled the government and economy, but it allowed a parliament to be elected. Women, however, were not allowed to vote. Only men who could trace their roots in Kuwait to before 1920 were allowed to vote. This policy meant that about 65,000 people —less than ten percent of Kuwaitis living in the country—were actually entitled to cast ballots.

In 1986, the emir suspended the parliament that had been elected the year before and imposed press censorship in an attempt to quiet opposition groups within the country. But pressure against the government continued, and in 1990 a National Council was created by the emir. This council could question government policy but was not allowed to pass laws of its own.

The invasion by Iraq gave new life to those opposing the autocratic government of the Sabahs. Many Kuwaitis had courageously fought against the invaders and now wanted a greater voice in the governing of Kuwait.

In the spring of 1991, seven opposition groups joined forces to protest the existence of the National Council and to demand that the old parliament be reconvened.

Following the liberation of their country, however, the Sabah family has moved very slowly—if at all—to bring greater democracy to Kuwait. Instead of reconvening the old parliament, the emir stalled for time and called for the election of a new parliament in October 1992. In a further effort to quiet opposition, the emir announced a proposal to give every Kuwaiti family $70,000 to help restore the losses suffered during the occupation.

Shiek Jabir-al-Ahmed al-Sabah, the emir of Kuwait, addresses members of the United Nations.

Opposite and below:
Black smoke fills the desert
as Kuwait's oil wells blaze out
of control.

Black Sky at Noon

When the wind blows in from the north, the sun shines. When it comes from the south, the sky is black at noon.

In the first months after the war, the fires from 640 burning oil wells cast a thick, choking blanket of smoke over Kuwait. Approximately five million barrels of oil—one tenth of the total oil used each day throughout the world—was going up in smoke.

Many scientists feared that the dense black clouds would reach the upper atmosphere and threaten the growing seasons throughout the region and even as far away as the Asian subcontinent. These clouds contained not only smoke but unburned particles of oil, gases, and soot.

Scientists were aware that in the summer the *shamal* winds blow across Iran, Iraq, and the Arabian peninsula. These seasonal winds blow in a southerly direction and carry the monsoon rains toward the Indian subcontinent. The monsoons are vital for agriculture throughout Asia.

In addition, the fires were creating a mist of soot and oil that threatened wildlife and fisheries in the Persian Gulf. Kuwait's fires had raised the carbon dioxide level in the atmosphere by two percent. On a daily basis, they were creating as much carbon dioxide as is produced by all the cars, homes, and industries of France.

On the ground, the burning wells created huge, gummy lakes of oil so thick that the desert could not absorb them. When the wind came in from the south, a smoky chemical bath doused buildings, cars, and people. When it rained, a greasy gray liquid fell for hundreds of miles.

To fight the fires, the Kuwaitis called in three American companies—Red Adair, Inc., Boots & Coots, and Wild Well Control. The Texas-based oil firefighters decided to first tackle the smokiest fires, which were near the airport in Kuwait City. They faced a difficult challenge. Some of the well fires had four hundred-foot plumes of flames and four thousand-degree temperatures that turned the surrounding sand to liquid. In addition, the Iraqis had packed the oil wells with deadly mines that would immediately explode when tampered with.

Slowly, well by well, the fires began to be put under control. By the summer of 1991, about 275 well fires had been extinguished. By November of 1991, the last major fire had reportedly been extinguished, ahead of the schedule.

But the long-range impact on the environment remained uncertain. In Qatar, four hundred miles south of Kuwait, it rained unburned drops of oil. In the mountains of Kashmir, thousands of miles away, the snow started to turn black.

The seven opposition groups were too divided among themselves to come up with a common program. Six months after liberation, the vote for women seemed as far away as ever and elections were only a hope for the near future.

Instead, all the people of Kuwait could hope for in the months immediately after their liberation was to rebuild their shattered economy.

The Struggle to Rebuild

Since Kuwait's economy was based on the sale of its oil, the oil-well fires set by Iraq were a devastating blow to the country. With hundreds of wells in flames, and the rest of the country in ruins, Kuwait turned to the United States for help. Soon, experts from America were in the Kuwaiti sand, extinguishing the towering flames. Each blaze that was put out represented one more step toward Kuwait's economic recovery. Although many fires had been put out in the first few months, oil-well workers did not expect the last flame to burn out until March of 1992.

By September 1991, Kuwait was already producing some 150,000 barrels of oil a day, which was enough to provide for its own needs and to begin exports to other countries.

But other parts of the economy were also in great need of help. The Kuwaitis were very slow in re-establishing many government ministries, so the U.S. Army Corps of Engineers had to restore electricity and water to the country. Non-oil businesses, however, were slow to recover, with one exception—automobile dealers did a thriving business as Kuwaitis hurried to replace the 250,000 vehicles stolen by Iraqis.

Business leaders were reluctant to rebuild until they got a better sense of the government's policy toward compensating them for the property they had lost to the Iraqis. The business community was also concerned about the size of the population of the country in the future. With the

A thick layer of oil covers a cormorant that has come ashore at Khafji, Saudi Arabia. The millions of gallons of crude oil that were intentionally dumped into the Persian Gulf have caused massive long-term destruction of the environment.

Palestinians being expelled, and with many Kuwaitis still living abroad, the future of the country's economy remained uncertain.

By the summer of 1991, Kuwait City often seemed like a ghost town. Traditionally, during the hot season, many Kuwaitis vacation in Europe. One member of the Sabah family was able to travel to Asia. When she returned, she had with her forty new Asian servants, who would replace her former Palestinian servants. In many ways, this was a symbol of the sense of priorities of the Kuwaiti government. It seemed intent on putting out the oil fires and punishing the Palestinians, but had little sense of what else to do to bring democracy to Kuwait and to restore its prosperity.

Chapter 4

Defeat and Defiance

The Persian Gulf War did not totally destroy the armed forces of Iraq, but it eliminated them as a threat to its neighbors. When the war began, about 610,000 troops—more than half of Iraq's army—were stationed in Kuwait. By the end of the war, the U.S. Defense Department estimated that 100,000 troops had been killed, 300,000 wounded, and 60,000 captured by the allies. The rest had deserted. These figures are guesses, and the true casualty rate may never be accurately known.

Iraq also lost more than four thousand tanks—all but a few hundred of its total tank force. The Iraqi air force had been neutralized early in the conflict when the Americans took command of the sky. About 120 Iraqi fighters fled the country to neighboring Iran, where they were promptly seized by the Iranians.

The air campaign against Iraq had caused civilian deaths probably in the thousands, but the exact number was never revealed by Iraq. Allied bombers attacked power plants, government and military buildings, telecommunications centers, bridges, and airfields. A major goal was to attack facilities that could aid Iraq in producing nuclear weapons. After the war, the United Nations discovered that Iraq's nuclear program as well as programs producing chemical and biological weapons were much larger than anyone had

The possibility of civil war in Iraq once again challenged Saddam Hussein's grip on power

Opposite:
Kurdish rebels wave their weapons after defacing a portrait of Saddam Hussein.

Saddam Hussein asks fellow Iraqis to forget political differences and work together for peace.

thought and that many of these plants had not been damaged in the bombing.

Iraq had suffered a humiliating military defeat. A democratic government could not have survived such a disaster, but the dictatorship of Saddam Hussein held onto power in the months immediately after the war. He did so despite a civil war that broke out as he was challenged by two major groups in Iraq—the Kurds in the north, and the Shiite Muslims in the south.

Civil War

The Shiites of southern Iraq. In the aftermath of the war, the southern part of Iraq—almost fifteen percent of the country's entire land area—was occupied by more than 100,000 allied soldiers. This desert area and the surrounding populated southern portion of the country is the home of Shiite Muslims. The Shiites make up more than half the population of Iraq. However, Saddam Hussein and his ruling Baath party are mainly Sunni Muslims, who form another branch of Islam.

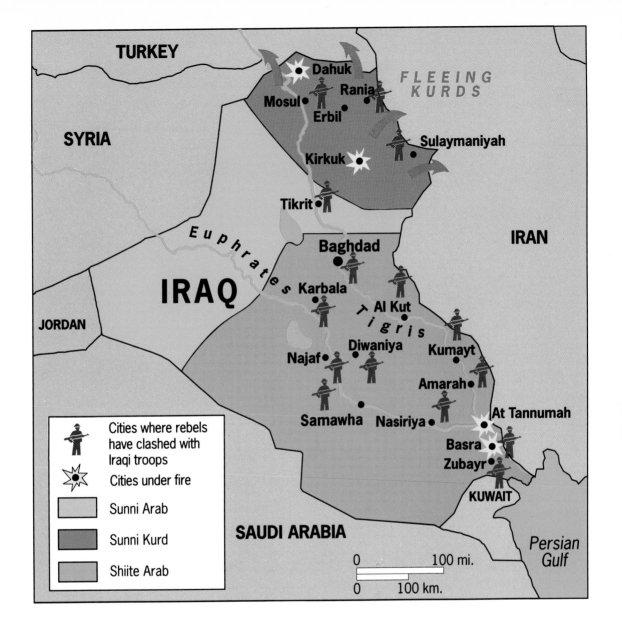

The Iraqi Shiites in the south were greatly influenced by neighboring Iran, whose population is largely Shiite. Sensing that Saddam Hussein had been weakened by the defeat in the war, the Shiites of Iraq rose in rebellion in the days immediately after the cease-fire. The center of the rebellion was the city of Basra, which is immediately north of Kuwait and on the border with Iran.

The revolt was not well organized, but it did receive support from Iran, which sent its own Revolutionary

The Shiites

The Shiites are members of one of the great divisions of Islam. Although Shiites live all over the Mideast, they are concentrated in Iran and Iraq. (The most sacred shrines of Shiites are at Karbala and An Najaf, in Iraq.) The Shiites of Iraq form a slight majority of the 18 million Iraqis, but the government is controlled by Saddam Hussein and his Baath party, almost all of whom are Sunni Muslims.

The division between Sunnis and Shiites began in the seventh century A.D. The schism occurred in a dispute over Muhammad's successors. The Shiites believed that Ali, Muhammad's cousin and son-in-law, and his two sons, Hasan and Husein, were the true successors.

All three were murdered, and a rival dynasty, the Umayyads, was established. Shiites, however, recognized eleven true successors to Muhammad who were not part of the Umayyad dynasty. The twelfth successor, or *imam,* is believed to be hidden, according to Shiite tradition. Shiites believe that the twelfth imam will appear on the world's last day.

Unlike the Sunnis, Shiite Muslims are far more zealous and strict in their beliefs. The Shiites believe that government should be run by high-ranking clerics (as is the case in Iran) and that women must cover themselves completely with a traditional garment called the *chador.*

Because of the intensity of their beliefs, Shiites will look for guidance to their religious leaders regardless of their nationality. The Shiites of Iraq, for example, looked to the government of Iran for spiritual guidance. Even though citizens

Shiite Muslims are far more strict in their beliefs than Sunni Muslims.

of Iraq, their spiritual loyalty was not to Saddam Hussein but to the Shiite government of Iran. The Iranians, in turn, provided arms and other support when the Iraqi Shiites rose in rebellion against Saddam Hussein in March of 1991.

Shiite populations also live in Lebanon, where terrorist groups— the major one called *Hezbollah*— have carried out kidnappings against Westerners and supported terrorist attacks against neighboring Israel.

Although the exact nature of Hezbollah's ties to Iran are not known, most observers believe that Iran exercises some influence over the group. The Iranians were most likely influential in the release of two Western hostages in August 1991.

The bond of Shiism remains strong throughout the Middle East, and Shiites believe that the clergy should control the government. Although most Arab governments are controlled by Sunni Muslims, who do not share the same belief, the power of Shiite influence stemming from Iran must always be taken into account.

Guard units into Iraq to aid in the battle. Shiite leaders freed political prisoners and then slaughtered government officials and suspected collaborators. In the city of al-Nasiriya, they hanged the mayor after gouging out his eyes and cutting off his nose.

Some Iraqi units retreating from Kuwait joined the rebellion, but eventually Iraqi forces loyal to Saddam Hussein were able to gain the upper hand. Using whatever tanks were left over, as well as artillery and helicopters, the Iraqi army blasted the Shiites in Basra and in other rebellious cities, including Karbala and Najaf. Tanks fired point-blank into homes, and civilians were struck by shells fired from helicopters. These missiles were loaded with white phosphorous, which causes severe burns. The slaughter on both sides was horrendous.

After a month of bloody fighting, Saddam Hussein reasserted his control over the southern part of his country.

The Kurds of northern Iraq. The northern part of Iraq is the home of the 4.9 million Kurds, who are not Arabs but are mainly Sunni Muslims. The Kurds of Iraq, who make up about a quarter of Iraq's population, have been fighting for a homeland of their own. In 1988, Saddam Hussein used poison gas against rebellious Kurds in the town of Halabja, killing more than five thousand.

Now, in the wake of the Iraqi defeat, the Kurds, like the Shiites in the south, rebelled against Saddam Hussein in an effort to claim their independence. By the end of March 1991, it looked as if the Kurds might succeed. A coalition of Kurdish political groups, called the Front of Iraqi Kurdistan, controlled the entire northern part of Iraq as well as the borders between neighboring Turkey and Iran.

But once the Shiite rebellion in the south was crushed, Saddam Hussein turned his weapons against the Kurds and attacked them with helicopter gunships, tanks, and loyalist troops. Kurdish strongholds of Kirkuk, Erbil, and Mosul came under strong attack. The battle quickly turned against the Kurds.

The Suffering of the Kurds

Fearing that they would be murdered by the Iraqis, some 1.5 million Kurds fled across the borders of Turkey and Iran in April 1991. Hundreds of thousands stayed within Iraq but retreated to the high mountains of the north, where they huddled in camps in freezing weather and with little water, food, or shelter. During this terrible period of hardship some seven thousand refugees died.

The United States and its allies refused to give military aid to the Kurds, even though many felt the Americans had encouraged the uprising. But as the conditions of the refugees worsened, a huge international effort was organized to ship them food to prevent mass starvation. In April, U.S. and allied forces entered northern Iraq and established a protective zone to shield the Kurdish refugees from the Iraqi forces.

A Promise of Autonomy

Once under allied protection, the two leading Kurdish leaders, Massoud Barzani of the Kurdish Democratic Party and Jalal Talabani of the Patriotic Union of Kurdistan, entered into negotiations with Baghdad to establish an agreement granting autonomy to the Kurds. Saddam Hussein's government agreed in theory to grant the Kurds autonomy but refused to include the oil-rich city of Kirkuk in the autonomous zone. In July the allied forces withdrew from northern Iraq and encouraged the Kurds to return to their homes in northern Iraq. Although some did, many preferred to remain in the north in a small United Nations protective zone, where they believed Saddam Hussein's forces would be unable to harm them.

Iraq's Weapons of Mass Destruction

One of the major reasons Iraq was seen as a threat to its neighbors was the fact that it had supported a program to develop nuclear weapons. One nuclear complex, at Thaji,

The Kurds of Asia

Country	Kurdish Population	% of Population
Iraq	4,900,000	26
Syria	1,400,000	11
Turkey	14,500,000	25
Iran	6,700,000	12
Soviet Union	400,000	less than 1%

Kurdish refugees crowd together at a camp in northern Iraq.

The Kurds: A People Betrayed

The Kurds are an ethnic group scattered among five countries of the Middle East. They are ethnically close to the Iranians and have been devout Sunni Muslims since the seventh century A.D. Although they have never been able to establish a homeland of their own, the Kurds have traditionally resisted domination by other nations.

In the late 1800s the Kurds were under Ottoman Turkish rule. At the end of World War I, they brought their claims for independence to the 1919 Paris Peace Conference. This conference, which resulted in the Treaty of Versailles, did nothing to establish a Kurdish homeland.

In 1925 and 1930 Kurds living in Turkey revolted against the government and were defeated. Kurds in Iran revolted periodically in the 1930s and were also crushed. Throughout the 1960s the Kurds in Iraq revolted against the central government, but they were repeatedly defeated.

On three separate occasions in recent times the Iraqi government reached agreements with the Kurds to grant them autonomy—in 1966, 1970, and 1984. In all three cases the Iraqis reneged on their promises. In 1988 the Iraqis used poison gas on the Kurds in the city of Halabja and killed five thousand.

Throughout their long history, the Kurds have been tough fighters. Tribal loyalties, however, have always prevented them from achieving the unity necessary to achieve autonomy or independence.

In the aftermath of the Persian Gulf War, the Kurds of Iraq tried once again to free themselves. During the war, President Bush had encouraged all the people of Iraq to overthrow Saddam Hussein. The Kurds now hoped the Americans would aid their uprising, but they were sadly mistaken. At the start of their rebellion in March 1991 the Kurds claimed to have 30,000 fighters called *peshmerga* ("those who face death"). But they were no match for the helicopters and tanks that Saddam Hussein used against them.

More than 1.5 million Kurds fled across the border into Turkey and Iran in the wake of their latest defeat. Hundreds of thousands of others endured terrible hardship in the high mountains of northern Iraq, where they had fled in fear of Iraqi retaliation.

But when the suffering of the Kurds brought outcries from around the world, a huge humanitarian effort was organized to help stave off starvation. U.S. and allied forces finally entered northern Iraq in order to shield the Kurds against the Iraqi army.

By the summer of 1991 allied troops were withdrawn but a UN protective zone remained to guard those Kurds afraid to return to their villages and towns.

After most of the fighting was over, the Kurdish leaders of Iraq—Massoud Barzani and Jalal Talabani—made an agreement with Baghdad granting the Iraqi Kurds more autonomy. It remained to be seen if the Iraqis would honor this

A Kurdish man holds the body of his daughter, killed by Iraqi forces during the uprising.

latest pact in a long history of betrayal.

By the fall of 1991, the Kurds once again became consumed in conflict. Large groups of refugees in southern Turkey began to rebel against the Turkish government. Ironically, help for the rebellions came from Saddam Hussein. Iraq began to supply Kurdish rebels with guns and other equipment. This time, Hussein was using the Kurds as a way to pay Turkey back for their opposition during the Persian Gulf War.

An Iranian soldier stands atop a mountain of guns turned over by Kurds fleeing to Iran for refuge.

near Baghdad, had more than one thousand buildings and covered an area as large as Washington, D.C.

During the war, the allies had bombed plants suspected of being involved in Iraq's nuclear program. After the war, the Iraqi government was supposed to give the United Nations a list of all material it possessed that could be used to make a nuclear bomb. It was also required to reveal all types, locations, and amounts of chemical and biological weapons. Under the terms of a U.N. resolution, Iraq had to agree to the destruction of all such weapons.

By the spring of 1991, however, it became clear to the allies that Iraq was concealing the true extent of its nuclear

An Iraqi truck containing nuclear equipment awaits inspection by U.N. officials at an unidentified site.

Iraqi army bulldozers destroy Scud missiles under U.N. supervision at Al Taji military camp in Baghdad.

program as well as the amounts of chemical and biological weapons that had survived the war. In an effort to find out the true extent of Iraq's weapons of mass destruction, the United Nations sent an observer team to Baghdad. Despite several attempts to make an inspection, the U.N. team was turned away and was even fired on by Iraqi forces.

Only after President Bush hinted that the allies might attack suspected weapons sites—and set a date of July 25 for Baghdad to live up to the U.N. resolution—did the Iraqi government reveal what it still had in its possession.

The news was disturbing. A substantial arsenal of chemical and biological weapons had survived the war. Nearly 10,000 nerve gas warheads, 1,000 tons of nerve and mustard gas, and nearly 1,500 chemical weapons bombs and shells still survived. The Iraqis also admitted they had lied about the true nature of a plant at Salman Pak, near Baghdad. Originally claiming it was a food-processing facility, the Iraqis admitted it was actually used to make biological weapons.

Iraq's Hidden Arsenal

When U.N. inspectors arrived unannounced at a top-secret Bagdhad government office in September of 1991, they found documents that confirmed their worst fears. Reams of material showed that Saddam Hussein was dangerously close (perhaps only months away) from having a nuclear bomb. This material also confirmed that much less of Iraq's arsenal had actually been destroyed by the war than was previously believed.

Understandably, the Iraqis were not eager to have inspectors seize these documents. When U.N. officials insisted, they were surrounded by armed guards in a Baghdad parking lot and held captive for four days while the world watched the stand-off. Finally, threats from Washington and the United Nations forced Iraq to back down. After analyzing the Iraqi material, weapons analysts were astonished at just how advanced Saddam Hussein's nuclear capability was. Whereas previous estimates put explosion of a crude Iraqi nuclear device anywhere from six months to ten years away, the new data indicated detonation was feasible in as little as two months.

Just what did the inspectors find?

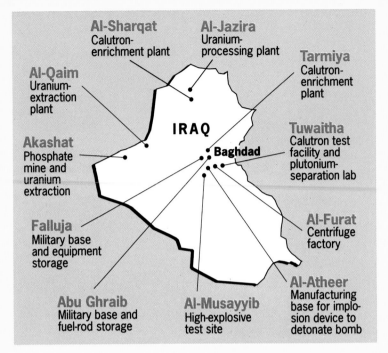

Al-Sharqat Calutron-enrichment plant

Al-Jazira Uranium-processing plant

Tarmiya Calutron-enrichment plant

Al-Qaim Uranium-extraction plant

Akashat Phosphate mine and uranium extraction

IRAQ

Baghdad

Tuwaitha Calutron test facility and plutonium-separation lab

Falluja Military base and equipment storage

Al-Furat Centrifuge factory

Abu Ghraib Military base and fuel-rod storage

Al-Musayyib High-explosive test site

Al-Atheer Manufacturing base for implosion device to detonate bomb

Plutonium and Uranium

Specially processed uranium and plutonium are used to set off a chain reaction in a nuclear fission bomb. At a reactor in Tuwaitha, U.N. inspectors found three grams of illegally produced plutonium. In Akashat, inspection teams turned up small amounts of weapons-grade uranium. Evidence of uranium and plutonium processing were also found at Al-Qaim and Al-Jazira.

Calutrons and Centrifuges

In order to be useful in nuclear weapons, uranium and plutonium must be enriched. One process uses a calutron, which is a device that employs electromagnets to separate fissionable (usable) uranium from non-fissionable uranium. Evidence of twenty-three calutrons was found in the material seized by U.N. inspectors.

A centrifuge also enriches uranium. This device extracts fissionable isotopes by spinning uranium compounds at super-high speeds in a rotating cylinder. U.N. officials say that Saddam Hussein had plans to build more than six hundred centrifuges.

More Hide and Seek to Come

In the future, inspectors will continue to perform surprise inspections of suspected nuclear facilities. More than likely, new confrontations and tense situations will arise. President Bush has already indicated that he will not tolerate continued interference from the Iraqis on inspection procedures. If Saddam interferes, Bush is prepared to take more aggressive measures to ensure thorough and accurate inspections. The president's plans include flying U.N. inspectors over Iraq in helicopters, sending Marine Corps escorts with the helicopters, deploying ground forces to attack and secure key Iraqi bases, and even launching a new strategic bombing campaign to destroy facilities that pose the greatest threat.

The allies had specifically avoided targets where biological weapons were believed to be stored. A hit by an ordinary bomb could have spread a deadly biological agent such as anthrax, across the region, killing millions.

Iraq also disclosed three secret uranium processing plants and admitted that its scientists had been able to create a small amount of plutonium from the spent fuel at one of its civilian nuclear reactors. Both uranium and plutonium are used to make nuclear bombs. By the fall of 1991, U.N. inspectors had uncovered secret documents and information indicating the existence of Iraqi weapons, facilities, and technology more advanced than anyone had guessed.

The existence of these weapons, even after the fury of the air war, created a difficult situation for the allies. While most members of the coalition were reluctant to resume the war, they also had few options to force Iraq to reveal the existence of nuclear sites and chemical and biological weapons. The one measure that had done the most harm—sanctions—seemed to hurt the people more than Saddam Hussein's government.

Sanctions

After the invasion of Kuwait, the United Nations adopted a number of sanctions against Iraq in order to force it to give up its aggression. The most damaging was the refusal to buy Iraqi oil.

Virtually all of Iraq's money came from the sale of its oil in the world market. Without these sales, Iraq would have reduced reserves of cash to buy weapons, food and other products, and spare parts for its military and its industries.

After the war, the sanctions began to be felt by the average Iraqi. With its electrical industry severely bombed, the country could not supply electricity around the clock. Without electricity, water purification plants could not operate and epidemics of cholera and other intestinal infections began to break out all over the country.

The United Nations and the Cease-Fire

In the days immediately following the August 1990 invasion of Kuwait, the United Nations Security Council condemned the invasion. Shortly thereafter, a series of severe economic sanctions were passed against Iraq. By forbidding foreign trade and financial transactions and by not allowing the Iraqis to sell their oil abroad, the U.N. hoped to force them to withdraw from Kuwait.

In December 1990, with Iraq still occupying Kuwait, the Security Council voted to authorize the use of force to eject Saddam Hussein's forces from Kuwait. The deadline for Iraq to leave was January 15, 1991.

The United Nations in New York City.

When the Iraqis failed to comply, the allies launched Operation Desert Storm, which ended six weeks later in the liberation of Kuwait.

In the aftermath of war, the United Nations continued to play a role to bring about a permanent cease-fire in the conflict and long-range peace to the region.

The cease-fire agreed upon at Safwan was temporary. Its main purpose was to set the conditions for an immediate end of the fighting. The Iraqis quickly agreed to the terms, which required them to end all resistance, to return to Iraq while leaving their weapons in place, and to refrain from flying all fixed-wing aircraft over their own country.

In April 1991, a permanent cease-fire resolution was passed by the Security Council over the bitter objections of the Iraqi delegate to the United Nations. This resolution sought to expand the conditions for peace and to guarantee that Iraq would never again be a threat to its neighbors. It called for Iraq to do the following:

• Reveal the extent and location of all its biological and chemical weapons and destroy them under U.N. supervision.

• Destroy all of its ballistic missiles under U.N. supervision.

• Turn over all materials that could be used to make a nuclear bomb to the appropriate agencies.

• Pay reparations to Kuwait out of future sales of its oil.

Only when these terms were met, would the economic sanctions that were passed in 1990 be lifted. The future role of the United Nations would be to monitor a demilitarized zone on both sides of the Iraq-Kuwait border.

The U.N. was also responsible for sending inspectors to Iraq whose job it was to verify Saddam Hussein's nuclear capability. But Iraq was not cooperative. By September of 1991, U.N. officials were still struggling to get access to vital nuclear information. It was only after an intense battle of wills that inspectors finally managed to seize some of the detailed information they needed.

The terms of the permanent cease-fire had still not been met more than six months after the end of the war.

M

MALTE

IRAN
(REPUBLIQUE ISLAMIQUE D')

U.N. members discuss the enforcement of sanctions against Iraq after the war.

Saddam Hussein's government claimed that the sanctions were preventing it from getting much-needed cash to buy medicines to fight the health emergency. The United States was skeptical, saying that Saddam Hussein's government had stolen billions in cash and gold, which it was saving for weapons purchases in the future instead of buying food and medicine for the people. Nevertheless, in July 1991, the United Nations agreed to a one-time sale of oil over a period of months in order to allow the Iraqis to get cash for civilian needs. Not happy with the conditions of the sale, Iraq refused the plan.

Throughout the summer of 1991 it was clear that the people of Iraq were being hurt by the sanctions. Hospitals were short of vital medicines and were filthy and fly-ridden; raw sewage flowed in the streets; electricity was available for only part of the day; and some areas of the country were severely hit by starvation.

But did Saddam Hussein allow such conditions to exist in order to crush opposition? The debate continued as the dictator managed to hang onto power despite defeat in battle and civil war on the homefront.

Chapter 5

Prospects for Peace

In the aftermath of the Persian Gulf War, the Mideast stood poised on what seemed to be the verge of a new era, one in which peace for the entire region seemed more possible than ever.

The United States had gained new influence as a result of the victory. Within days of the end of the war, U.S. Secretary of State James Baker began a series of trips to the region to explore the possibilities for peace throughout the Mideast. His main goals were (1) to preserve Iraq as a nation but to make sure that it would never again be a threat to its neighbors and (2) to begin a peace process between Israel and the Arab states of the region. A settlement between Israel and the Arab countries would, the Americans hoped, include a final resolution of the question of a Palestinian homeland.

The Palestinians claimed a right to a homeland on the same territory that made up the state of Israel, including the occupied West Bank of the Jordan River. The major Palestinian organization, the PLO, had always refused to recognize the right of Israel to exist. However, in the late 1980s the PLO reversed itself and acknowledged the existence of Israel. Despite continuing acts of resistance on the part of Palestinians and terrorism both within Israel and without, hopes were high by 1991 that the Israelis and

The war created some new alliances and made meaningful negotiations for peace a real possibility

Opposite:
U.S. Secretary of State James Baker greets King Hussein of Jordan as they met to discuss longterm peace in the Middle East.

Palestinians would soon begin the long process of negotiating and settling their dispute.

The war had led to a shake-up of politics and power throughout the region. But there were still many players, and some were ancient enemies. Each of their interests would somehow have to be satisfied before any overall settlement could be reached.

The Soviet Union, the only other world superpower, was no longer an important influence in the Mideast. Under Mikhail Gorbachev the Soviets had opposed Iraq's aggression against Kuwait. And because of their own internal economic and political problems, the Soviets were no longer a reliable source of weapons and other support for their allies in the Mideast, especially Syria. With the collapse of communism and the disintegration of the Soviet central government in August 1991, it fell to the United States to use its influence to pursue a plan for peace.

The Gulf States

The Gulf states of Saudi Arabia, Oman, Bahrain, Qatar, and the United Arab Emirates had gained the most from the war. They had taken the risk of allowing the allies to use their soil to launch air, naval, and ground attacks against Iraq. The victory brought them closer to the United States and made them more willing to support U.S. policies in the region.

Although they had always opposed Israel, in practice the Gulf states adopted a live-and-let-live attitude. Now, after the war, the United States pressed them on two fronts. The first was a call for their support for a Middle East peace conference to settle the question of a Palestinian homeland and to end the long conflict between the Arab states and Israel. The second was to set up a regional security system that would allow these states to defend themselves from future aggression and prevent the need for another war fought by American and allied forces.

By August 1991, the United States had withdrawn seventy percent of its equipment and all but 44,000 troops from Saudi Arabia and Kuwait. The Bush administration continued negotiations with its Gulf state allies for new security arrangements that would allow some American forces and equipment to remain in the region, especially in Saudi Arabia and Kuwait.

Israel

The Israelis had heeded the American request and not retaliated against Iraq when Scud missiles fell on their cities. In the aftermath of the war, Secretary of State Baker now pressed them to agree to a regional peace conference. The Israeli government of Prime Minister Yitzhak Shamir was extremely reluctant to attend such a conference. The Israelis did not wish to give up the lands they had occupied since the 1967 Arab-Israeli War—the West Bank (disputed with Jordan), the Golan Heights (disputed with Syria), East Jerusalem, and the Gaza Strip.

Although they had agreed to grant some form of autonomy in the future to Palestinians living within Israeli borders, the Israelis were adamantly opposed to the creation of a Palestinian state in the West Bank. Such a state, they believed, would seriously threaten their existence.

But Baker continued to press the Israelis. Realizing that their support in the U.S. Congress might diminish and that the U.S. aid that was vital for the Israeli economy and military might be cut, the Shamir government reluctantly agreed to attend a peace conference.

However, the Israelis insisted on the right to approve the Palestinian delegation that would attend the conference. In particular, they refused to allow any Palestinian to attend who was a resident of East Jerusalem. To allow such people to attend, the Israelis maintained, would be to admit that all of their capital of Jerusalem did not belong to Israel.

Nor would they talk to anyone who was a member of the Palestine Liberation Organization, which the Israelis considered a terrorist group bent on the destruction of Israel. Instead, the Israelis insisted that only West Bank Palestinians be included in the delegation that would attend the conference.

Baker attempted to work out a compromise that included East Jerusalem Palestinians attending first as "observers" and then being included in any later sessions by vote of the original participants.

The Israelis were still refusing such a compromise as late as September 1991, one month before the conference was scheduled to convene.

James Baker toasts with Israeli Prime Minister Yitzhak Shamir during a March visit to Jerusalem.

ISRAEL TODAY

LEBANON

GOLAN HEIGHTS

SYRIA

Sea of Galilee

Mediterranean Sea

WEST BANK

Jerusalem●

Dead Sea

GAZA STRIP

ISRAEL

JORDAN

EGYPT

☐ **Disputed areas now occupied by Israel**

| 0 | 40 mi. |
| 0 | 40 km. |

Gulf of Aqaba

SAUDI ARABIA

James Baker attended a meeting of Arab foreign ministers in Riyadh soon after the war ended. Ministers from Saudi Arabia, Syria, Egypt, the United Arab Emirates, Bahrain, Kuwait, and Qatar all participated in peace discussions.

The PLO and Jordan

The Palestine Liberation Organization and Jordan were the big losers in the Mideast poker game. Jordan, once an ally of the United States and a moderate Arab state with regard to Israel, had backed the Iraqis. Scud missiles aimed at Israel had flown over Jordanian territory. The United States was angry at Jordan's King Hussein for not backing the allied effort. After the war, Jordan had to bear the crushing burden of hundreds of thousands of Palestinian refugees expelled from Kuwait, who now flocked to squalid refugee camps along its borders.

The PLO had also backed the wrong side. As the peace conference began to take shape, PLO Chairman Yassir Arafat demanded the right to pick the delegation that would represent the Palestinians. But the Israelis refused outright, and no compromise seemed evident by the late summer of 1991.

Syria

Syria turned out to be a potentially big winner in the aftermath of the Persian Gulf War. Although a hardline, anti-Israeli (and therefore anti-U.S.) state with suspected ties to international terrorism, the Syrians had joined the coalition against Iraq because of their hatred and fear of Saddam Hussein's power. In the wake of the war, Syrian President Hafez al-Assad did an about-face and agreed to negotiate directly with Israel, as long as the Israelis agreed to return the Golan Heights.

Even though the Israelis flatly refused to do so, Assad supported the idea of a peace conference. Why had this long-time opponent of Israel changed his mind? In his meetings with Baker, Assad realized that the United States now called the shots in the Middle East. The Soviet Union had supplied all of Syria's economic and military aid during the 1980s. But as the Soviet Union began to disintegrate under the pressure of its own internal economic and political disorder, that aid began to dry up. The only other source was the United States. In order to become a full-fledged client of the United States, the Syrians realized they would eventually have to make peace with Israel.

The Role of Iran

In some ways the most mysterious player in the Mideast in the aftermath of the war, Iran turned out to hold many cards. Bitter enemies of Saddam Hussein, the Iranians had fought a bloody and inconclusive war with Iraq between 1980 and 1988 that left a million Iranians dead.

They now rejoiced at Saddam's humiliation and did everything in their power to assure that he would never be a threat to them again. Their support of the short-lived

Shiite rebellion in southern Iraq did not lead to Saddam's downfall, but the Iranians had other plans.

Following the death of their radical leader, Ayatollah Ruholla Khomeini in 1989, Iran's government sought to improve its relations with the West. The Iranians now realized that they needed Western aid to rebuild their economy in the wake of the Iran-Iraq War. In order to gain favor in the West, the Iranians exerted pressure on Shiite groups in Lebanon who had been holding American and other Western hostages, some for as long as six years.

In August 1991, two of the hostages—John McCarthy, an Englishman, and Edward Austin Tracy, an American—were released as a gesture of goodwill, apparently through the influence of the Iranians. In an effort to secure a release of all the hostages, U.N. Secretary General Javier Perez de Cuellar began a series of negotiations that involved the Israelis releasing Shiite Palestinians detained in Israel in return for release of all the remaining American and Western hostages. By the fall of 1991, those negotiations began to pay off. On October 22, American Jesse Turner was freed and the future looked brighter for those hostages that still remained.

An October Peace Conference in Madrid

In July 1991, Baker was able to get all parties to agree to a peace conference, which was to convene in October. All participants had to agree to some compromises.

The Israelis wanted a conference that lasted for only one session and then would disband. The Arabs wanted many different sessions. The Baker compromise called for an opening meeting that all parties would attend. Then the conference would break into smaller groups in which the Israelis negotiated with individual Arab states.

The Arabs wanted the conference to be sponsored by the United Nations. The Israelis wanted no U.N. involvement at all. The Baker compromise called for a conference sponsored by the United States and the Soviet Union. A

Javier Perez de Cuellar, U.N. Secretary General, speaks to reporters after a meeting with Iraqi Foreign Minister Tariq Aziz in Amman, Jordan.

U.N. observer would be present but would not be allowed to participate.

But who would represent the Palestinians? With the Israelis insisting on only West Bank Palestinians and the PLO and other Arab states insisting on PLO participation, this difficult issue hung over the prospects for peace in the aftermath of the Persian Gulf War.

What the Future Holds

Making predictions about the future of the Mideast roller-coaster has never been an easy task. There are so many disputes to solve and so much bitterness among the Mideast players. Still, James Baker managed to achieve enough compromise and cooperation to set his 1991 peace conference for October 30, in Madrid. It was the first time in seventeen years that Arabs and Israelis sat down at the same table together. That meeting alone showed just how much the world had changed and, despite the tragedy of the Persian Gulf War, how 1991 turned out to be a year in which hope was once again alive in the Mideast.

Chronology: 1991

FEBRUARY

- Allied forces begin ground war with attack on Kuwait and Iraq (February 24).
- Iraqi forces collapse after 100-hour battle (February 27).
- President George Bush announces that "Kuwait is liberated." (February 28).

MARCH

- Iraqi military leaders meet with Gen. H. Norman Schwarzkopf in Safwan, Iraq, and agree to terms of temporary cease-fire (March 3).
- Last of allied prisoners of war released (March 6).
- Iraqi Shiites in southern Iraq rebel against the government of Saddam Hussein, but are defeated by the end of the month.
- Kurds in northern Iraq begin revolt against Iraq.
- Government of Kuwait begins to return from exile in Saudi Arabia.
- First American troops begin to return home from war zone.
- U.S. Secretary of State James Baker begins first of several trips to Middle East to arrange for a peace conference between Israel and Arab states.

APRIL

- Kurdish rebellion defeated by Iraqi army.
- About 1.5 million Kurds flee to border areas of Iran and Turkey and to high mountains of northern Iraq in fear of Baghdad's retaliation.
- U.S. and allied troops enter northern Iraq to protect Kurdish refugees.

MAY

- Humanitarian effort to bring food and medicines to Kurdish refugees begins.
- Kurdish rebel leaders begin negotiations with Baghdad on autonomy.

JUNE

- Kurdish leader Massoud Barzani reports that Iraq has approved a draft agreement providing for elections for an autonomous legislature in Kurdish lands of northern Iraq (June 23).
- Americans celebrate U.S. victory with parades in major cities across the country.

JULY

- Syria accepts U.S. proposals for a peace conference with Israel to be held in October. Israel says it will attend but insists on right to approve make-up of Palestinian delegation, which would include no East Jerusalem Palestinians (July 18).
- U.S. and allied troops complete withdrawal from occupied zone of southern Iraq.
- Demilitarized zone along Kuwait-Iraq border is set up, monitored by U.N. observers.
- U.N. team is fired on by Iraqi troops when they try to inspect Iraq's nuclear program.
- Iraq reveals the extent of its nuclear and chemical and biological weapons programs after President Bush says allies might use force (including bombings) to eliminate weapons of mass destruction (July 25).

AUGUST
- U.N. Security Council votes to continue sanctions against Iraq but agrees to allow Iraq a one-time sale of $1.6 billion worth of oil to be used to buy food and medical supplies (August 7). The offer is rejected.
- Two hostages in Lebanon—John McCarthy, an Englishman, and Edward Austin Tracy, an American—are released. Hopes rise that a deal to free remaining Western hostages in Lebanon can be worked out through mediation of United Nations.

SEPTEMBER
- U.N. inspectors detained in Baghdad parking lot after taking possession of documents containing information about Iraqi nuclear weapons and facilities.

OCTOBER
- American hostage Jesse Turner is freed on October 22.
- The first direct negotiations between Arabs and Israelis in seventeen years begins at a Mideast peace conference in Madrid, October 30.

For Further Reading

Bratman, Fred. *War in the Persian Gulf.* Brookfield, CT: Millbrook Press, 1991.

Childs, N. *The Gulf War.* Vero Beach: Rourke Publishing, 1991.

Frey, James S. *Iraq* (World Education Series, 1988).

Gordon, Matthew S. *Islam.* New York: Facts On File, 1991.

Iraq. New York: Chelsea House, 1988.

Mulloy, Martin. *Kuwait* (Let's Visit Places and Peoples of the World series). New York: Chelsea House, 1988.

Pimlott, Dr. John. *Middle East: A Background to the Conflicts.* New York: Franklin Watts, 1991.

Index

Acknowledgments and photo credits

Cover, p. 16: ©Chip Hires/Gamma-Liaison; p. 4: ©G. Merillon, Chip Hires/Gamma-Liaison; p. 6: ©B. Markel/Gamma-Liaison; p. 8: ©Greg Gibson/Wide World; p. 10: ©John Gaps III/Wide World; p. 12: ©Ed Reinke/Wide World; p. 13: ©T. Ashe/Gamma-Liaison; p. 14: ©John Rice/Wide World; p. 15: ©Salah Naswari/Wide World; p. 17: ©John Chiasson/Gamma-Liaison; pp. 19, 25: ©David Longstreath/Wide World; p. 20: ©Cynthia Johnson/Gamma-Liaison; p. 22: ©G. Bassignac, G. Saussier/Gamma-Liaison; p. 24: ©Bill Haber/Wide World; pp. 27, 42: ©Martin Nangle/Wide World; p. 29: ©Vogel/Gamma-Liaison; pp. 30, 33: ©Greg English/Wide World; p. 31: ©Roberto Vorea/Wide World; p. 34: ©ABC Ajansi/Gamma-Liaison; p. 36: ©Luc Saint-Elie/ Wide World; p. 38: Wide World; p. 41: ©M. Daniels/Gamma-Liaison; p. 43: ©Mohammed Sayaad/Wide World; pp. 44, 45: ©H. Arviddson/ United Nations Photo; p. 48: United Nations Photo; p. 49: ©Quidu Noel/Gamma-Liaison; p. 50: ©Youssef Allan/Wide World; p. 54: ©Nati Harnik/Wide World; p. 56: ©Sadayuki Mikami/Wide World; p. 59: ©Bassignac Gilles/Gamma-Liaison.

Maps and charts by David Bell.

Special thanks to Cindy Dopkin and Elvis Brathwaite.